Horse Training

Engaging In Circular Movements, These Dressage
Workouts Aim To Enhance Lateral Suppleness With Ease

*(The Comprehensive Guide To Raising And Caring For
Rocky Mountain Horses)*

Arthur Drouin

TABLE OF CONTENT

Arabian Bio 1

Never Trust a Cheap Piece 14

Bio of a Friesian Horse 40

Interesting Horse Facts 56

Horse Owner Mistakes 90

UP TO 12 MONTHS OF TRAINING YOUR FOAL NEWBORN 101

Behavioral Issues and Training 132

Arabian Bio

You have an Arabian horse of your own. That is fantastic because Arabs are eager to train loyal horses. Getting to know and instruct your new best friend will be great fun. But before you can properly teach an Arab, you should educate yourself on a few aspects of the breed. The Hot-blood category includes several breeds, the Arabian horse being just one. Hot-blooded horses have a lot of energy and a low boredom threshold. They'll need care, exercise, and excitement. Their lively and loving nature makes these Arabs popular choices for family pets. Don't be alarmed by the unfavorable reputation of a hot blood horse.

Even though these horses can be demanding regarding food and space, they make generally wonderful pets. If you are bringing your Arab into a small herd, be cautious about introducing them gradually and avoid pressuring any animal to become friends with another. Arabs are horses of a medium stature; some are shorter than fifteen hands. They belong to the lower heights of the horse family, in actuality. A breed of horse native to the Arabian Peninsula is known as the Arabian or Arab horse. It is also one of the oldest breeds, having 4,500-year-old archaeological evidence of horses resembling contemporary Arabians from the Middle East. Arabian horses have been utilized to enhance other breeds by bringing speed, refinement, endurance, and strong bone, which have spread throughout history. Several contemporary riding horse breeds have Arabian ancestry.

The Bedouin people were nomads and valued the Arabian, which originated in a desert environment. It was frequently placed inside the family tent to provide cover and prevent theft. The ability to build great relationships with humans was one of the attributes that led to the selective breeding of a kind, obedient, and easily taught horse breed. The Arabian also acquired the necessary vigilance and great spirit for a horse. This mix of eagerness and sensitivity compels current Arabian horse owners to treat their animals with expertise and respect.

The Arabian breed is adaptable. Arabian horses still compete today in many other equestrian sports, including endurance riding, where they are the dominant breed. They are one of the world's top ten most popular horse breeds. They are currently present worldwide, spreading to the Middle East, continental Europe, South America, the United States, Canada, and the United Kingdom.

The naturally high tail carriage and comparatively long, level croup, or top of the hindquarters, are other distinguishing characteristics. Arabians must meet the USEF breed standard for solid bone and proper conformation. A deep, well-angled hip and a relaxed shoulder are common among Arabians.

Not all Arabians have 17 pairs of ribs instead of the typical 18, and many, but not all, have five lumbar vertebrae instead of the typical 6.

Arabians make extraordinarily devoted friends. They show their loved ones affection and are gregarious and lively. Your Arab could need some time to warm up because they can be reticent around new people. When properly socialized, they generally get along with dogs and children. Even though some people dislike or negatively perceive these horses, you can be sure that they can make wonderful companions. They are quite simple to train due to their extreme intelligence. Training this breed shouldn't be too hard. They enjoy being among others and can get very unhappy if left alone for an extended period. However, be cautious because these horses are often startled and may unintentionally step on your foot. These horses are routinely turned in because they are hot-blooded or have an erratic fear reaction. Because this breed was originally bred for endurance or combat, exercising caution and respecting their energy level is critical.

Past Events

The oldest tangible evidence of the Arabian horse in Ancient Egypt is a skeleton discovered in the Sinai Peninsula that dates to 1700 BC and is believed to have been delivered by the Hyksos Invaders.

The Arabian horse greatly influenced the history of Islam and the Middle East. Muslim influence spread throughout North Africa and the Middle East by 630.

In 1854, Egyptian breeders imported horses reared on the Arabian Peninsula and Palestine's deserts as the foundation bloodstock.

Most likely, starting in 1095, the first horses with Arabian ancestry to reach

Europe did so indirectly via Spain and France with returning Crusaders.

To address the ongoing demand for breeding Arabians as a source of pure bloodstock, two members of the Russian nobility founded Arabian stud farms around 1889.

Notable imports from Arabia to Poland took place between 1743 and 1812.

Between 1519 and 1540, 250 horses with Arabian-like ancestry arrived in the Americas, most likely in Mexico.

Founded, recording roughly 71 animals, and by 1994, the number had reached half a million. There are reportedly more Arabians registered in North America today than worldwide.

What to Expect from Arabian Dog Training: Arabian dogs are incredibly simple to train. All you have to do is show that you are the dominant horse. To demonstrate to your Arab who is in control, begin teaching and discipline him immediately. Start as soon as you get him home in the horse trailer. He'll try hard to get your approval and swiftly recognize you as the leader. Depending on the Owner and the Arab, the procedure can take anywhere from a month to more than a year. It matters that you are living each moment to the fullest and that your main goal is to ensure that the Arab is doing the same.

Make sure your Arab is prepared to ride and already saddle-broke before selecting. Look for one who looks to like you and is already friendly. More than 90% of the Arabs bought in the US have already received this level of training. By the time they are two years old, most Arabs are saddled.

The majority of Arabs that are bought are five years old or older and have had several years of saddle time. Note that this book is meant to train your Arab companion to be your best friend and most dependable, not teach you how to saddle-break an Arab. They don't know anything about you when you buy your Arab. They're unaware that you now consider him your own and aspire to be his closest buddy.

Arabs usually don't require a lot of strict discipline. If your dog misbehaves, you can quickly "check" him by pulling on the lead rope while wearing a halter and holding the rope. He will learn not to engage in behavior once you demonstrate why it is undesirable.

To make sure your Arab develops into a regular, well-rounded horse, you want to socialize him. You ought to keep him engaged as well. Boredom is a typical issue that people have with Arabs. Strange behaviors like "cribbing" (chewing on a fence rail), pacing, or "weaving" back and forth might be developed by a bored Arab.

You may ensure that your Arab has as much pasture time as possible if you own the horse property where he resides and you also live there. You should budget $200.00 per month for full pasture board and up to $600.00 per month for full care, which includes a stall, paddock, and daily pasture time if you "board" your Arab at a nearby stable.

If your primary goal is a showhorse, we do not advise you to keep your Arab in a stall with a short turnout time. The majority of Arabs find such kind of confinement intolerable. Exercise vigorously and let him run in his pasture or turnout to keep him moving. To make sure he is more focused throughout training, give him some exercise. It's a good idea to start teaching your Arab by bringing him out of the stall on his rope and halter after he's had a few days to adjust to his new home. Start by giving him some basic instructions as you guide him. You'll be amazed at how quickly your Arab learns once you give a command, such as "Walk, stand, walk, stand."

Never Trust a Cheap Piece

With no rate for the turn, he flew into the first barrel. The large brown gelding with racing heritage was as free-spirited as any horse I had ever ridden. I was on the verge of losing my cool as the barrel approached.

"Keep it together. You know he doesn't rate, but you must trust that he will turn."

I was unable to complete it.

My thoughts were racing, "It's too fast, too fast, he won't make the turn," and my pulse was pounding.

I finally had to follow my gut and attempt to get him to slow down, so I kept my hand out as long as possible.

Yes, he did.

He took a hard seat on his ass. It resembled striking a brick wall. He lost speed as he slowed down and skillfully avoided the first barrel. We took the initial turn, even though it would take more time! Hurry on to the second and third now!

An eight-year-old sorrel gelding who had never raced barrels in the competition had a nice maiden run. Less than a second slower than the winner of his debut race. He was prepared to begin his work. Nobody will ever comprehend the difficulties he brought forth. A horse that could not lope well in a lead six months prior.

After failing to stop a short, stocky paint horse from bucking, I needed to find something manageable. My acquaintance knew someone attempting but wasn't having much luck to head on a large, racing-bred sorrel gelding. Someone tried to make a trade. They believed they could use the little paint for roping after they rode him. I adored their horse's lineage. He had been on the track and was bred to run. A long-legged gelding with the thin muscling of a thoroughbred. The horse wasn't acting like much of a heading horse, and as I saw them attempt to rope, I could tell that he wouldn't have had much cow in him until you fed him a hamburger. Most likely, we both felt we came away with a better horse than the other.

The labor ahead of me was unknown to me.

To put it mildly, my first ride was an intriguing one. He was a bit of a prick, but I knew that before. He loped off at a trot. There are no issues there. Then, the issue surfaced. He took off like a rocket when I told him to lope to the right, straight down the arena's left side. As if to get me off his back, he banged my leg against the fence. When I believed I had him under control, he ran away from me while I struggled with him to set myself free. We took the left lead and headed down the arena.

What on earth occurred just now?

How did this gelding learn to fight hard to stay to the left?

It was going to require some consideration, I guess.

Alright, let's get started.

I would ask him to lope after I circle to the right daily. He used to sprint towards the barrier. I would stop him and then get back to work. He kept doing this workout nonstop for over a week until he eventually caught up and avoided running over the fence. When he did, I halted him by making a half circle. Well done, boy! Let us expand upon that.

We could easily lope a circle to the right in two more weeks.

It's time to begin barrel training now.

Leads were difficult to catch on cue, but only momentarily. He began to gain confidence when he discovered he could easily navigate around the barrels. We quickly started running the pattern and increasing the speed.

These days, I begin working a horse on the barrels with a simple bit. Once I have them going, I use exact responses from a bit that they appear to enjoy and with which they function well to fine-tune our partnership.

I adore fragments.

I have a lot of bits because I have trained many horses, but I couldn't find anything I liked for him. I tried one and got a good rate, but it didn't bend. Another was too supple in the curves and weak to stop the strong man when he started to run.

So, I went shopping.

Although there was a good amount of choice in the tack store I went to, my cheap ass had to dig through the sales bucket. It was there. $5 gets you a straight bar bit. An excellent deal for something I wanted to try but didn't have. Later on, if I liked it, I might purchase a more costly version.

Let me just add that that $5 amount nearly put me in the hospital for a very big bill!

I gave it a try at home.

He loved it, and it worked beautifully.

Coincidentally, I received an invitation from my neighbor down the road to come workhorses. I saddled him up and went to where I intended to ride him. I prepared to take off running. I was so happy to demonstrate my strides with this horse that I confidently took off.

I felt the reins come loose halfway around the second barrel.

Has my curb chain broken? Alright, let's just complete the run.

I watched the entire thing slide out of his mouth around the third barrel!

"Oh no!"

I immediately felt bad about choosing to manage my money conservatively. This horse enjoyed bolting. My thoughts were racing. What on earth was I supposed to do? My neighbor's arena opened into her pasture. "I have to stop before then, or we're going to wind up in the woods," I warned myself.

Then it dawned on me: I got it! He would be aiming at the fence if I could just persuade him to shift slightly to the left. I would leap off, and he would have to slow down to duck left or right.

Yes, ladies and gents, I was a goat tyer, and I had my broken $5 bit hanging at my horse's chest while I planned a goat-tying escape at ninety kilometers per hour!

Most people would probably not have selected my particular technique, but not everyone would think that trying to get off before heading out of the back of the pen is the only choice.

I think I gave my neighbor and everyone else there a serious scare that afternoon.

I managed to get off, albeit not entirely upright. There was a small roll present. I managed to get the far more costly variant of that bit, and the gelding proceeded to produce a lovely barrel horse for a young girl who never gave it a thought that he might not turn.

I still don't even look at the clearance bins in tack stores!

Fundamental Instruction

Basic training starts early in a horse's life, much as in the first two phases. If a horse was trained correctly from the start, he wouldn't require this kind of instruction in the future. Basic training includes "breaking" to help the horse accept his rider.

The horse can walk, trot, and lope under control at this point. Here, one is also taught how to turn left and right. He will comply when the horse learns to slow down or regulate his stride and senses pressure on his legs. Horses trained under a riding discipline will pick up the skills necessary to stop, slow down, and accelerate.

This is also the age that most horses are "backed." Backing differs from breaking in that the former requires you to get on the horse's back. A horse can be backed without necessarily having to move or be ridden; it can just be sitting on.

The entire process of educating horses to ride is called breaking. This includes teaching horses to remain composed and not become alarmed by the legs or motions of a rider. A horse is referred to as "green broke" when this occurs, but as he gains experience and adjusts, he will develop into a "well broke" horse.

The age at which a horse is first trained to ride or put in the saddle varies depending on the breed and discipline. Riding many stock horse breeds starts at two years old. As early as the fall of their first year of training, many Thoroughbred racehorses are conditioned to accept light and small riders. At two years old, horses intended for harness work are often trained to have a cart positioned behind them. Some horses are even trained to pull a light cart at two, even though they won't be ridden until they are three years old. This will help them develop stronger muscles and better attitudes.

Most horses worldwide, in all disciplines, are ridden for the first time at three. The breeds that mature more slowly are the lone exception, and they aren't trained to ride until they are four years old.

The horse should be fearless around people. They should view riding as merely another lesson to be learned. When saddled, horses with proper foundation rarely rear, buck, or flee.

Older horses never trained to ride can pick up the skills. Their age may make it take longer, but it is still feasible. As long as elderly horses are accustomed to people and don't have any undesirable behaviors, training them is not too difficult. It is exceedingly difficult to train a horse rescued from the open range and entirely feral. A domesticated horse that has come to despise people is the hardest to train.

Training in Western Discipline

Discipline training has numerous subcategories, which will be covered later. As the horse's rider refines and perfects training, this stage lasts many years. Western discipline training includes rope, reining, team penning, western pleasure, trail riding, pole bending, and ranch horses.

Training in English Discipline

Most trainers just concentrate on teaching English or Western discipline. English pleasure, show jumping, dressage, cross-country jumping, and endurance are among the disciplines offered by the former. A horse can be taught multiple classifications by its trainer.

The Diverse Equine Specializations

attire

If you watch the Olympics, you may be familiar with dressage, but this elegant fusion of art and sport dates back deeper. Dressage combines the strength of gymnastics with the beauty of ballet for both the rider and the horse. All eyes are on the Musical Freestyle section of dressage competitions, where the rider choreographs a ride of moves to music.

tenacity

In contemporary endurance sports, the horse and rider aim to finish a course quickly. Participants can anticipate covering 50, 75, or even 100 miles in a single day.

Hunting Foxes

Tracking a red fox with foxhounds or other scent hounds is the customary method of fox hunting. A master of foxhounds commands a following that follows him either on foot or by horseback.

Parade Pony

Parade horses are exquisite and fashionable animals. They ought to be elegant and pleasing. The horse needs to walk with animation when it is displayed. Maintaining proper etiquette is essential when aligning and performing movements. Since this sport is about beauty, horses should be in excellent shape.

Driving for Fun

There are events in this sport wherein ponies or horses are mounted on replicas or real vintage cars. This competition is divided into numerous groups based on the vehicle type, the horse size, and the number of horses (singles, pairs, tandems, or unicorns) used to tow the vehicle.

Pole-bending

Six poles are put in a line in pole bending, and the horse and mounted rider weave around them. A strong horsemanship is necessary for pole bending to be successful.

Racing

There have been horse races for millennia. This horse sport has a long history in our society. Standard-bred horses race in harnesses rather than under saddle, but thoroughbred horses travel great distances quickly.

Regaining control

Reining competitors require their horses to run a pattern. Large quick circles, rollbacks over the hocks, little slow circles, 360-degree spins when stationary, and flying lead changes are a few examples of these. Points are awarded to horses based on their attitude, authority, smoothness, rapidity, and finesse when performing the various movements.

Rodeo

Rough-stock and timed events comprise professional and competitive rodeo. The latter comprises riding a bull bareback and on a saddle bronc. Activities offered by the former include barrel racing, tie-down roping, team roping, steer wrestling, and steer roping.

Display Leaping

In jumping contests, the horse and rider are put to the test via a variety of conditions on an obstacle course. This evaluates the rider's horsemanship and the horse's talent, freedom, and obedience when jumping.

Penning Team

This brief competition takes a team of three riders 60 to 90 seconds to identify and divide three distinct animals out of a huge herd. The goal is to place these animals in a pit at the opposite end of the arena.

Riding on Trails

Trail riding is the term for biking on unpaved routes. Trail rides take place outside, as opposed to enclosed arenas. These could be casual get-togethers for one person or a small group but also big events.

Keeping Safe

This fun and competitive sport combines gymnastic and dance moves performed on a cantering horse. The performances are so captivating that many people have come to see this event.

A horse can be trained for many more disciplines. Recall that mastering a single discipline requires years of practice, regardless of the option you select for your equine companion.

Bio of a Friesian Horse

You recently acquired a Friesian horse. This is fantastic since Friesian horses are devoted and willing to learn. Getting to know and instruct your new best friend will be great fun. But before properly teaching your Friesian horse, you should educate yourself on a few facts regarding the breed. They'll need care, exercise, and excitement. Because of their kind and carefree nature, Friesian horses are considered perfect family companions.

Although they can be demanding regarding food and space, Friesian horses generally make wonderful pets. If you bring your Friesian horse into a small herd, introduce them carefully, and don't push any animals to be friends. Some Friesian horses are under 16 hands tall and very athletic. They vary from 15 to 17 hands, depending on the specific horse you select.

It was circa 4000 BC that horses were first tamed. The domesticated horse is thought to have become common around 3000 BC. Horses fall into three major types. Hot-blooded horses, including Arabians and Thoroughbreds. Morgan horses and Quarter horses are examples of warmbloods. Draught horses, like Clydesdales and Friesian horses, are considered cold blood.

Among other things, the stocky, powerful legs, expressive head, prominent eyes, robust hindquarters, and strong, arched neck of the Friesian horse breed are well-known traits. They appear to be very strong and capable. It is well known that Friesian horses possess courage, strength, intellect, a positive attitude, endurance, and vitality.

Past Events

The Friesian horse is one of the most traditional breeds used today. The Friesian horses of today are invariably black. The Netherlands is where the Friesian Draught Horses originated in the fourth century. The Friesian Horse was often nicknamed a Belgian Black. One thousand five hundred pounds was the largest Friesian horse weight. The tallest Friesian is 17 hands tall. Two Friesian Horses could draw heavy carts as Draught Horses. Although they are still used for work, Friesian horses are also utilized as dressage horses, show horses and recreational riders.

The Friesian horse has long been used for riding, but it was first bred as a working horse. The Friesian Horse gained its greatest notoriety as a War Horse, capable of carrying a knight in full armor for a whole day. The Friesian always performed exceptionally when wearing a harness and towing a carriage or cart with big loads. The contemporary Friesian horse makes a fantastic riding horse. The Friesian horse has demonstrated aptitude in dressage and horse competitions. Worldwide, there are about 45,000 Friesian horses.

What to anticipate from a Friesian horse's training

Training a Friesian horse is rather simple. All you have to do is declare yourself to be the leader. To establish who is in authority, begin training and discipline your Friesian horse immediately. Start as soon as you get him home in the horse trailer. He'll try hard to get your approval and swiftly recognize you as the leader. Depending on the Owner and the Friesian Horse, the process might vary and take anywhere from a month to more than a year. It matters that you are living each moment to the fullest and that your main goal is to ensure that the Friesian Horse does, too.

Be sure to select a saddle-broke, ride-ready Friesian horse when making your selection. Look for one who looks to like you and is already friendly. More than 90% of Friesian horses bought in the US are already trained to this level. Most Friesian horses become saddle-broke around two to three years old.

Most Friesian horses bought are five years old or older and have had some saddle time. Please be aware that this book teaches you how to educate your Friesian horse to be your closest and most dependable friend—not how to saddle-break one. Your Friesian horse doesn't know anything about you when you get it. They're unaware that you now consider him your own and aspire to be his closest buddy.

Friesian horses usually don't require a lot of strict training. If your dog misbehaves, you can quickly "check" him by pulling on the lead rope while wearing a halter and holding the rope. He will learn not to engage in behavior once you demonstrate why it is undesirable.

To make sure your Friesian horse develops into a regular, well-rounded adult, you should socialize him. You ought to keep him engaged as well. Boredom is a typical issue that individuals have with Friesian horses.

Strange behaviors like "cribbing" (chewing on a fence rail), pacing, or "weaving" back and forth can be developed by a bored Friesian horse.

You may ensure that your Friesian horse receives as much pasture time as possible if you own the horse property and reside there. When boarding a Friesian horse at a nearby barn, For complete pasture board, you should budget $200.00 per month; for complete care, which includes a stall, paddock, and daily pasture time, you may spend up to $600.00 per month.

Unless your primary goal is to have a show horse, we do not advise you to keep your Friesian horse in a stall with a short turnout time. That degree of captivity is intolerable for the majority of Friesian horses. Exercise vigorously and let him run in his pasture or turnout to keep him moving. To make sure he is more focused throughout training, give him some exercise. It's a good idea to start training your Friesian horse by bringing him out of the stall on his rope and halter after you've allowed him a few days to adjust to his new home. Start by giving him some basic instructions as you guide him. When you give a command like "Walk, stand, walk, stand," you'll be surprised at how quickly your Friesian horse picks it up.

Cherish your Friesian steed!

Chapter 8: Guidance on Horse Grooming

Grooming your horse is a wonderful opportunity to check for injuries and get to know them better. Grooming your horse before and after each ride is a good idea. This is an excellent time to examine your horse's hooves for any debris or stones that could cause discomfort.

Using a curry comb on the horse's coat to remove dirt is usually the first step in grooming. When brushing your horse's legs, you should use a soft brush instead; if your horse likes it, you can also use the soft brush on its face. Wipe your horse's eyes and nose with a moist sponge. A comb can be used to comb the mane and tail.

Cutting Off Horse Ears

Horse clipping is a crucial aspect of horse maintenance, and the ears are one body region often overlooked when trimming. Clipping your horse's ears around once a month is a good idea, although most individuals would only think about doing so before entering a horse show. Regular ear cutting reduces the hair clumps parasites like to nest in.

Cutting Off Ears:

First, wash your horse. Ensure you eliminate all the debris and as much oil and loose hair as possible.

If the amount of filth within the ear is substantial, clean it; if not, don't mess with it.

Your horse should be led to an appropriate location for clipping after being put in a halter with a lead rope.

It will require patience to clip ears because many horses are afraid of clippers. The horse should first be accustomed to the loudness by having the clippers close to its face. You might need to keep doing this for a few days until your horse relaxes if they are really unhappy.

Before trimming the ears, you should clip the mouth, whiskers, and bridle path if you will clip everything.

When creating the ears, fold the sides together until the tips contact; at this point, you can cut from the base to the tip.

Ensure the back of the horse's ears is clipped, and the animal can remain motionless.

On the opposite ear, carry out the identical procedure. Be cautious not to adjust the clippers' settings so that one ear is longer than the other!

You might purchase clipper spray to ensure that the clippers aren't overheated or dry. Applying this between cutting the first and second ears works well.

To prevent the horse from losing some of its natural defenses against inner ear issues, only clip a few inches along the inner arc of the ear using the horse clippers.

Knowing Your Horse

Because they are habitual creatures and respond well to regimentation, horses are highly clever animals that can pick up new skills fast if they are given the patience to do so.

In any case, horses respond best when they feel linked to their rider; to succeed in training, a horse must trust its rider; therefore, building a relationship with your horse comes first.

They have personalities like people; therefore, you need to know your horse's thoughts. Is it a shy horse that needs encouragement and care? Is it a brazen and disobedient hose that requires a lot of restraint and moderation? Or is it a submissive steed, willing to obey commands?

Before beginning the program, you must accurately understand this material.

There are various ways to build a bond with your horse, but the most obvious is to touch them physically. You can use your hands, whips, spurs, or saddle, depending on what makes your horse comfortable or uncomfortable.

With this knowledge, all you need to do is understand that horses react by seeking comfort or avoiding discomfort. A rider who understands their horse will concentrate all their training efforts on helping the horse feel comfortable.

A horse's response to discomfort will not be favorable; it may become completely terrified or unresponsive.

Horses have evolved into swift creatures because they have a strong innate desire to avoid danger. They would almost always choose to flee if given the choice, which is why horses are swift.

Remember, get to know your horse and what it finds comfortable or uncomfortable, and you'll have the essential knowledge required to train it!

Interesting Horse Facts

Horses are affectionate creatures by nature and want to please their owners.

There is some Arabian horse DNA in every Thoroughbred Horse.

In short distances, some thoroughbred horses have been recorded at 43.97 miles per hour.

Horses are excellent in combined training and show jumping.

Many former racers have wonderful careers such as dressage horses, youth shows, and family horses.

Larger horses are frequently utilized in hunter-jumper and dressage sports.

Polo ponies are smaller horses used for polo.

Nowadays, the Horse is most frequently employed as a racehorse, in rodeo events, as a show horse, for cutting and reining, as a ranch horse, or as an all-around family horse.

Section Three

Getting Your Horse to Socialize

How to Train Your Horse to Get Along with Others

With all of them

It's crucial to socialize your Horse from an early age. Are you aware of the reason? A horse that has received proper socialization will not be hostile or afraid of people or dogs. He is aware that both people and dogs exist and do not always threaten his safety. Conversely, an unsocialized horse perceives the world as a threat and responds accordingly. The presence of people or other canines frightens and threatens him. Therefore, you must begin socializing your Horse when you bring him home. Acclimate him to living with pets and other people.

Viewpoint (Yours)

Your Horse can see right through your attitude. You are like a book to him. He can tell when you are angry with him. Additionally, he can detect when you are upset and won't accept that it isn't related to him. As a result, you should always be forceful and have a positive attitude while socializing. When your Horse senses your positive energy, they will bond more easily. Be kind, loving, patient, and supportive at all times.

Express your pride and joy more than your annoyance or dissatisfaction. If you are frustrated, take a moment to breathe deeply and do something different with your Horse. When you're feeling composed, go back. Your secret to success when teaching your Horse will be positivity. Avoid pushing your Horse too much or losing your temper, as this can negatively impact your training experiences and overall outcomes.

Training your Horse to become the kind of Horse you want him to be when riding him later is a major component of socializing him. The initial several months of his training form him into the

Horse he eventually becomes. As a result, you should put in the most effort and concentrate on your final objective during this time. Therefore, ensure you have a strategy, follow it, be consistent, and be clear about what you expect from him. When he follows your instructions, show genuine happiness and excitement by rewarding him generously for his good behavior.

You'll be astounded at your ability to teach your new Horse if you adhere to these principles. Creating the unique connection you wish to have with your Horse for the rest of his life is a significant component of socializing. This can only be accomplished by showing him you are the herd's leader.

However, you also want to let him know you are best friends and love him. Your Horse will grow up to be the most devoted and caring buddy you have ever had if you follow the proper training methods recommended in this manual and immediately treat him like a best friend. When you approach social situations, act as though you want to be friends with this Horse, but don't forget to assert your authority as the group's leader and dominating friend. Maintain your firmness while remaining soft. Give instructions without being harsh or aggressive. Aggression is never a better socialization strategy for horses than firmness.

When & How to Introduce Your Horse to Others

When your Horse was only a few hours old, he started the socialization process. He interacts with his mother and, if any other horses are available, a few horses until then. A horse cannot simply expect his mother to teach him how to ride well. The Horse must be exposed to people and trained to interact with them from a young age. Mainly because your Horse's development is greatly influenced by this period of his life, which is also the most impressionable; your Horse is a bit older when you accept him in your life, so don't worry about your efficiency in training him. All it will take is a little more time from you. You must treat your Horse correctly as the alpha when you acquire him. Talk to him, touch him, and move his body. Get him used to being handled by humans. Each time you remove him from his stall, give him a brush. He'll discover that you're harmless, that this is fun, and that he can trust his new human herdsman. Introduce your Horse to a variety of settings. Take him on rides outside or stroll along a path with lots of grass, plants, animals, and other people strolling, exploring, and having picnics. Take him to your neighborhood lake, the beach, a stream, a pond, etc. Here's the main idea. Play around with it, be imaginative, and show him a variety of environments, including beaches, trails, and natural surroundings. Depending on your situation, he might be exposed to a slow-moving car if you have to go along a gravel road to reach a trail.

Noise, such as traffic, airplanes, trains, and cars, could be heard by your Horse. He will grow accustomed to the various settings and noises he encounters. You might need to transport your Horse in a trailer if you bring him to different locations. This teaches him that curiosity is okay instead of fear of many unfamiliar and unusual things. A good horse is a worldly one.

Allow your friends to meet your Horse when you bring them around so he can become accustomed to them and learn to enjoy a variety of people. You don't want him to grow unduly dependent on you to the point that he starts to doubt other people. Your Horse will bring you both closer together, so spend a lot of time developing your relationship with it. It also teaches him how to behave with you and others in an appropriate and inappropriate way. It tells him that you are a kind, dependable owner who values him and that spending time with you is joyful and enjoyable. It's a good idea to locate and develop various mentally and physically demanding activities to keep him interested and busy. Note: It's vital to allow your Horse some alone time. This helps him learn that it's okay to be nervous when you're not around to form a bond. Let him graze alone in his paddock or pasture for at least an hour or two a couple of times a day. Please do not approach him, whether by himself or with other horses.

To stop undesirable habits from developing early on:

Don't be hesitant to correct your Horse.

Tell him "No" forcefully if he nips your arm.

When he fidgets when being touched at the hitching rail, tell him "No."

Early instruction on what is acceptable and unacceptable can help him become a more obedient horse and reduce the need for corrective action in the future.

He will learn that you are in charge and that he must pay attention to you if you stop any negative behavior and start a positive one in its place. Believe it or not, he craves this from you. Start by telling him what actions are appropriate and what are not. Be stern but not mean.

Steer clear of shouting and physical punishment; these behaviors can permanently traumatize your Horse. You want him to respect you with pride in his heart, not to be terrified of you. To discipline your Horse and change behavior, all you have to do is say "No" with firmness and redirect them to something else to do. Now, it's time to start lightly teaching your Horse. Naturally, we go into great detail about that in this book on horse training.

Chapter 2: Training Behavioral Horses

Now that you have a good understanding of physical training, it's time to think about behavioral training as well.

Getting a horse does not mean you must start riding it immediately. Horses are not vehicles that require command without prior relationship building. When riding, you must interact with the

Horse to control its speed and ability to turn. This implies that both must understand the common language between the two parties. Any miscommunication between the rider and the Horse can result in unpleasant, if not dangerous, incidents.

For this reason, it's essential to teach your Horse to comprehend a variety of orders so that you and other riders can ride the Horse comfortably and without difficulty or misunderstanding. Ground training is the primary training technique used to transmit the behavioral knowledge that every Horse should possess. Trainers employ a variety of ground exercises to help their horses better understand typical commands and scenarios.

Untrained horses typically fear a variety of objects in our environment. Because of this, the Horse must learn how to live in harmony with its surroundings while maintaining composure. If a horse is readily agitated by everyday elements in their surroundings, it should be no surprise that a frightened horse may hurt the rider or trainer. Horses should be frequently trained in the usual demands of their field of application after receiving basic communication and behavioral training. This is another crucial consideration. Because dressage horses must perform different tasks, their behavioral and communication training programs will differ significantly.

In the following sections, we'll examine several facets of ground training and typical exercises used by trainers with horses.

Ground training is the primary way of educating young horses to shape their behavior and language of communication. To help the Horse comprehend these crucial lessons, older horses who have not received the proper training or lack certain behavioral skills are put through a similar training regimen. When training a young horse, groundwork helps to strengthen its frame without adding too much weight to the rider or trainer. The Horse picks up valuable intellectual lessons and continues its physical development.

Yearning

This method of training horses involves moving an untrained, green hose in a circle, with the trainer positioned in the center. Although longeing often uses a rope that the trainer holds and attaches to the Horse, it is also typical to see trainers not utilizing a rope. The Horse is then managed by the trainer by body language, noises, motions, and light rope tugging. The trainer will employ a range of cues during logging exercises to get the Horse to slow down, accelerate, and turn around, among other things.

One of the most crucial training techniques for improving a horse's comprehension of human body language is longeing. The trainer must refrain from forcing the Horse to run in a single direction during these exercises since the animal could grow too accustomed to it and stop trying to run or turn in the other direction.

Young horses are taught several aspects of communication through longeing. Longeing exercises are typically used to acquaint horses with various riding accessories, such as reins and saddles. Another use for longeing is getting a horse used to its rider. The rider acclimates to the Horse in a supervised setting for safety reasons. Exercise for horses that shouldn't be ridden is another use for it.

The Proper Leg Aids and Your Legs

Every riding horse should be able to withstand the rider's lower leg pressing against them. If the legs are too much for them, the rider's inappropriate leg positioning, kneeling, sharp boot edges, pulled-up heels that constantly scrape the Horse's sides, or improper spur usage could cause pain or discomfort. A motionless hind leg, supported solely by its mass, does not cause discomfort to the equine. The length of the rider's leg, the Horse's depth, the kind of saddle, girth, riding boot, etc., all affect how much the lower leg makes contact with the Horse's side. The Horse's legs ought to be loose and extended around its sides.

When the legs out of the stirrups hang long and loose, the stirrup length and leg posture in the full seat are correct, and finding the stirrups just requires turning up the toes. It is best to ride with shorter stirrups until muscles have fully stretched and strengthened, then gradually lengthen them to the proper position; otherwise, it will only look nice, and applying a leg assist will be quite challenging. Every time a person sits on a horse, they should ride without stirrups for a few minutes to stretch their muscles and increase their ability to ride longer.

Squeezing the Horse's sides with the calves will become difficult if the knees are gripped, as this would force the seat out of the saddle. Immediately behind the perimeter is the lower leg.

The knees are firmly in contact with the saddle in the light seat. The foot is gently twisted outward at the ankle, and the heel is firmly pressed down. The stirrup is under the ball of the foot, and the foot rests on the inner side of the stirrup.

The ankles do not touch the Horse's side. Rather, the calf and knee sit close to the Horse's side due to the foot's small inclination, providing the required grip for a stable, independent seat.

The leg help the rider uses to ask the Horse to move is called "forward-driving." It is employed to request that the Horse proceed, accelerate, extend his stride, regulate his speed, and slow down.

Since the perimeter is the most sensitive region of the Horse's barrel, the lower leg should apply the aid slightly behind it for maximum effectiveness. The rider's leg returns to a quiet, neutral mode, and the impulse is applied equally with pressure from both legs; the Horse should not need to answer questions again as soon as it replies appropriately. Ideally, once your horse moves and you've established the pace, he stays there until you give him a different order.

Pose of the legs "at the girth."

The forward-driving leg aid is the first leg assistance a rider should teach a young horse. Riding a horse will always need work; additional teaching and training will be more challenging if the animal is not attentive to this aid.

The hands permit the forward motion rather than impede it during an uphill transition or forward help, while the leg gently prods or vibrates to encourage the Horse to advance. The hands contain the forward action, causing the Horse to slow down by using his more engaged hocks, and the downward transition aid is a "dead" squeeze with the leg, pressing his hind legs more underneath him. To enable the Horse to distinguish easily between the two orders, the upward and downward leg aids must be distinctly different.

When you ask your Horse to move forward sideways—like leg yielding or a half-pass, you employ the "lateral-driving" leg assistance. In addition to stepping forward and sideways, the Horse is asked to move away from the leg pressure. The leg extends a little bit behind the girth. The moment the Horse's hind leg lifts off the ground on the side opposite the planned action is when the leg should nudge, not exert constant pressure. For instance, place your right leg on the Horse as soon as his right hind leg lifts off the ground when requesting his leg to yield to the left.

Section 1

Bio of the Andalusian Horse

You have an Andalusian horse of your own. That's fantastic since Andalusian horses are devoted and willing to learn. Getting to know and instruct your new best friend will be great fun. To understand how to educate an Andalusian horse best, you should first become somewhat knowledgeable about the species. They'll need care, exercise, and excitement. Because of their laid-back and loving nature, Andalusian horses are often considered perfect family companions.

Although they can be territorial in their food and space, Andalusian horses generally make wonderful pets. If you are bringing your Andalusian Horse into a small herd, be cautious about introducing them gradually and avoid pressuring any animal to become friends with another. Some Andalusian horses (mares) are under 15 hands tall, slender, and athletic. Indeed, the range of hands varies based on the specific Horse you select, from 14.3 for mares to 15-16.2 for all males.

It was circa 4000 BC that horses were first tamed. The domesticated

Horse is thought to have become common around 3000 BC. Horses fall into three major types. Hot-blooded horses, including Arabians and Thoroughbreds.Andalusian horses and Quarter horses are examples of warmbloods. Draft horses like Belgian horses and Clydesdales are considered cold blood.

The Andalusian horse breed is recognized for its graceful, powerful legs, expressive head, large eyes, hindquarters, and arched neck. They appear to be very strong and capable. Andalusian horses are renowned for their wit, bravery, kindness, endurance, and energy.

Past Events

The Andalusian Horse is one of the more traditional breeds that is still popular today. The Andalusian breed's DNA indicates that a "Sorraia" horse was one of their ancestors. There is also a combination of hefty European and Oriental horses in the Andalusian breed. The Oriental Horses, regarded as Hot-blood and distinguished for their intelligence and endurance, include Arabian, Akhai-Teke, Barb, and the now-extinct "Turkoman Horse."

The Andalusian Horse has been a part of the Iberian Peninsula for thousands of years. It is thought to have been a recognized breed for about 700 years. It doesn't seem to have altered much over the ages. About 185,000

Andalusians were anticipated to be registered worldwide in 2010.

Throughout history, the Andalusians have served as war horses. They have since excelled in bullfighting, stock horses, show jumping, dressage, and driving. Movies have made considerable use of Andalusian horses.

What to anticipate from Andalusian horse training

Training Andalusian horses is a pretty simple task. All you have to do is declare yourself to be the leader. To establish who is in charge, begin training and discipline your Andalusian Horse immediately. Start as soon as you get him home in the horse trailer. He'll try hard to get your approval and swiftly recognize you as the leader. The duration of the process varies based on the owner and the Andalusian Horse, ranging from a month to more than a year. It matters that you are living each moment to the fullest and that your main goal is to ensure that the Andalusian Horse feels the same way.

Ensure the Horse you select for your Andalusian is saddle-broke and prepared for riding. Look for one who looks to like you and is already friendly. More than 90% of Andalusian horses bought in the US are already trained to this degree. Most Andalusian Horses are saddle-broke when they are around 2-3 years of age.

Most Andalusian horses bought are five years old or older and have had some saddle time. Note that this book is about training your Andalusian Horse to be your greatest and most dependable buddy, not about saddle-breaking one. They have no idea who you are when you buy an Andalusian horse. They're unaware that you now consider him your own and aspire to be his closest buddy.

Generally speaking, Andalusian horses don't require a lot of strict training. If your dog misbehaves, you can quickly "check" him by pulling on the lead rope while wearing a halter and holding the rope. He will learn not to engage in behavior once you demonstrate why it is undesirable.

To make sure your Andalusian Horse develops into a regular, well-rounded adult, you should socialize him. You ought to keep him engaged as well. Boredom is a typical issue that individuals have with Andalusian horses. Strange behaviors like "cribbing" (chewing on a fence rail), pacing, or "weaving" back and forth can be developed by a bored Andalusian horse.

You may ensure that your Andalusian Horse has as much pasture time as possible if you own the horse property and reside there. You should budget $200.00 monthly for full pasture board and up to $600.00 per month for full care, including a stall, paddock, and daily pasture time if you "board" your Andalusian horse at a nearby stable.

Unless your primary goal is to have a show horse, we do not advise you to keep your Andalusian Horse in a stall with a short turnout time. That kind of imprisonment is intolerable for the majority of Andalusian horses. Exercise vigorously and let him run in his pasture or turnout to keep him moving. To make sure he is more focused throughout training, give him some exercise. It's a good idea to start teaching your Andalusian Horse by bringing him out of the stall using a rope and halter after adjusting to his new surroundings for a few days. Start by giving him some basic instructions as you guide him. You'll be amazed at how quickly your Andalusian Horse picks up new commands once you give them, such as "Walk, stand, walk, stand."

Horse Owner Mistakes

The first mistake is assuming you can mount any horse.
Horses are not all the same. Some will simply get you into the car so you can ride along. Some are quite safe for the environment, but you risk getting hurt if you don't ride much or at all. Older horses tend to be the ones that can rally virtually anyone. They will be the most understanding of errors a novice may make because they are ridden the most. Unless they are entirely broke, younger horses are more difficult to ride.

Mistake #2: Assuming only one method to train a horse exists. When seasoned equestrians have concerns about their horses, they search for solutions and pose inquiries. A book is among the first things they see. New horse owners assume that the training methodology described in this book is the same method all trainers employ. After attempting this method, owners of new horses typically conclude that their horse is stupid or untrainable because they cannot train their new mount.

Training a horse can be done in a variety of ways. Therefore, you should try a different technique if the one you're employing doesn't seem to work. You can find books or videos made by different trainers, who frequently employ a different approach than your own.

Error #3: Not Getting Enough Rides
If you're a novice horse owner and your horse is giving you trouble, it's likely because it needs to be ridden more frequently rather than breaking down. To become a good rider, a horse must be ridden frequently. Riding your horse is, therefore, the finest thing you can do for him. It is insufficient to ride a horse every two weeks.

Error #4: Assuming that the horse is to blame for mishaps. Horses are just like all other animals. They are dealing with issues. You'll frequently find that the horse's owner is mostly to blame for the troubles. To determine the situation's causes, you must examine matters about horses. You may be unable to control the individual you need to control in many situations. There are several methods available to you for creating controls.

Mistake #5: Owners lack comprehension of how horses think. Horses think differently from cats or dogs since they are not like those animals. Since horses are prey, anything that frightens them will cause them to flee. They have had this "flying instinct" for thousands of years. Horses are inherently terrified of practically everything; training them will require much patience and understanding.

Error #6: Novice equestrians are unaware that every encounter with a horse is a teaching opportunity.

You are training him, whether touching, brushing, or simply grooming him. Since your horse is similar to your child, he will pick up things from you as a novice horse owner. Therefore, you must take the time to reflect on what you do and how you do it. You may be surprised to learn how much of an impact you have on your horse's behavior.

Error #7: It will be more detrimental than beneficial if you are a novice horse owner and have never ridden a horse before.

Many novice horse owners will ride without any prior experience or knowledge. Comprehending your riding routine is critical because horses react to cues like leg pressure, saddle position, and rider nervousness.

Gaining knowledge of your horse is essential for riding successfully. Taking a riding lesson and learning how to ride a horse is preferable if you aren't already proficient at it. To acquire a nice horse, you also need to know how horses think, how to effectively train them, and how to ride regularly.

5. Ride Safely: The Rider Needs to Recognize Theirself and the Horse

Like the general public, some horseback riders stress excessively, while others appear overly carefree. Being at the spectrum's extremes when riding a horse can lead to various issues. For example, the overly carefree rider might never be ready for an emergency, and the anxious individual might work herself into a sufficiently pessimistic frenzy to make her horse feel as nervous as she does.

The finest riders are alert to their surroundings while being relaxed. Riding a horse often means being ready for someone or something else to alter your surroundings and put you and your horse in danger, just like operating a car.

Take the footing, for instance. Since not all horses have flawless footing, the rider may need to alter their direction while traveling due to obstacles like mud, hills, and rocks.

Aware riders pay attention to various elements of their surroundings, including vehicles, machinery, loose horses, and other riders. They think the weather could bring new challenges for the horse, such as a breezy day whirling plastic bags or billowing tarps. A vigilant rider understands that a herd of deer or straggling canines could surprise both them and their equine companion when they are on paths. A vigilant rider understands that there's a chance someone could accidentally slam it shut while they're in the ring.

Anything can divert your horse's focus from you at any time; it could be a malfunctioning vehicle, a barking dog, or a loud thunderclap. In addition to being ready to handle any issue as it comes up, the rider's awareness and comprehension of the possibility of disturbance in his surroundings also require him to maintain his horse's focus and prevent the horse from reacting to the best of his abilities.

Additionally, it frequently refers to the fact that when a horse responds to his surroundings, he is in the right area rather than the incorrect one. For instance, you should maintain a safe distance from other horses in the riding arena and be able to locate every horse using your peripheral vision. Ask someone to please move further away if they are passing too close. Why? Being ready could prevent another horse from running into yours if a truck backfires and spooks another one.

Of course, this does not imply that your horse will never flinch. It could catch you both off guard if a herd of deer breaks through the bushes ahead of you and your horse. But the difference between a horse that just stops and snorts with a start and one that spins around and runs home may be ascertained if your horse has been paying attention to you and you were prepared to handle such a reaction.

While riding and unwinding, pay attention to your surroundings, maintain your horse's focus, and be ready for anything unforeseen. This way, neither you nor your horse will be genuinely surprised, and you can prepare yourself to handle the situation to the best of your abilities.

Chapter 3: Getting Your Horse Back Home

Now that you've finished the initial phase of choosing and buying your ideal equine, it's time to take on the responsibilities of a horse owner. It makes sense that you will be both excited and anxious about the possibility, so a thorough strategy will help you calm your fears. This chapter will teach you what to do when your horse reaches home and the necessary duties involved in getting it there. Recall that your equine is transitioning into unaccustomed and novel environments. Thus, it is imperative to guarantee its safety and comfort.

Things to do before your horse returns home

Make sure your horse has some sort of shelter before it gets there. You can lodge the horse on your property or in a nearby stable if you have adequate acreage. Before the horse arrives, you must clean and check if the stable is on your land. Nothing dangerous should be inside the gates, stall walls, or fence, and they should all be in good shape. The stall shouldn't be very small or cattywampus to prevent your horse from feeling confined. Reducing your horse's nervousness is crucial because this is a new setting for them. If the fence is outside, especially an enclosure, ensure it is visible and the right height for the horse. You must take all necessary precautions because your horse may attempt to jump the fence. The horse should be able to be held inside the stall by a strong, sturdy door. Make the necessary queries if you intend to board your horse at a nearby stable to guarantee that it will be cared for safely and comfortably.

Checklist for Ready Stable

☞ Pick a suitable shelter ☞Sanitize and check the stable ☞Make any required repairs ✔Get the required equipment

The definition of "necessary equipment" varies depending on why the horse is being raised, but there are several things that every horse owner has to have.

- Feed and water basin.
- Head collar and lead rope
Bit, bridle, and saddle.
- Splint and tendon boots.
- Horse grooming kit. A curry comb, water and body brush, sponge, hoof oil, fly repellant, mane comb, and sweat scraper should be included. For convenience, you can place them all in one box.
- First aid package. Be prepared to care for your horse in an emergency or injury before the veterinarian arrives. Bandages, cotton wool, tweezers, scissors, wound cleaning, antibiotic spray, thermometer,

and veterinary emergency numbers should all be included in your first aid bag.

Immunizations

Make sure your horse has a comprehensive examination from a licensed veterinarian. Ideally, one should be experienced with the breed before bringing it home. Horses can receive a variety of immunizations to help them stay healthy. Even before your horse gets to your house, you, as its owner, must safeguard it by ensuring it has all the necessary vaccinations. If not given proper care, horses may become sick from illnesses or infections. You must take care of your horse for it to depend on you.

Revisit the Immunization Schedule

✔ Acquire the relevant vaccination information for horses.

☞ Have your horse checked out in-depth.

☞ Ensure your horse is immunized.

Feeding It is advisable to obtain all the information about your new horse from the former owner if your horse has one. Find out what kind of feed your horse likes to eat and how much hay it needs daily. Before bringing your horse home, buy its feed and hay. Do not push your horse to eat feed you do not want them to consume. Rather, introduce the feed gradually; over time, you will gain his trust.

All breeds of horses require water. The daily water consumption of an ordinary horse is approximately seven gallons. For this reason, you must make sure your horse has access to clean, fresh water. Your horse may respond adversely to drinking unfamiliar water since it is unfamiliar with your surroundings. Using the same basin, or one identical to it, that your horse is accustomed to is one strategy to combat. If they are not familiar with them, it may take some time for your new horse to get used to any automated water systems in your stable or barn. You will need to supply clean water at that time in a method your horse is accustomed to, like a basin or tub.

UP TO 12 MONTHS OF TRAINING YOUR FOAL NEWBORN

As I mentioned, I start getting ready when I touch a pony. I have a dream for every foal I consider brought into the world. Please aid yourself in recalling the completed thing.

Before you begin, know exactly what kind of horse you need. I have seen some beautifully put-together, well-reproduced ponies that should have been amazing but were destroyed because someone "ruined" them. An aware, willing pony for quite a long time of joy; alternatively, a nasty, pushy pony with 'qualification' concerns.

After my babies are engraved, I give them to their mothers to benefit from for a while. I do not get them and 'play' with them daily, nor do I wear bridles.

In the unlikely event that Mum was taken care of before the foal was produced, I continue to feed her and ensure the foal doesn't become used to switching feeds. While the foal is being transported for a snack or for Mom to have a feed, it might receive a peck on the bum or a few pictures, but that's all!

I NEVER USE HALTERS DURING THE FIRST FEW MONTHS WITH MY FOALS.

I have learned of so many foals that were abandoned in the yard or enclosure with their straps on, allowed to dangle or suffer serious injuries from getting hooked up on walls and trees, all so their owners could take care of them without having to buckle under the weight of the foals. Sounds unforgiving; here's the reason.

They should be trained to release stress before foals are purposely or otherwise connected to anything. They can get scared and typically want to flee, not realizing that the tension will eventually go away when they relax. They will freeze if they find themselves hooked on a tree or fence.

When my foals are four months old, I start assisting them in taking the lead. This is the first step in learning how to let go of pressure.

Educating your colt to take the lead in a Mareeba, Queensland show. Model: Samson

First, learn to appreciate the notion of your new foal and know when to give it a hard and when to let it go. At that time, every variety in the middle shares three fundamental characteristics.

Nature No. 1: the kind spirits, the wise ones; Nature No. 2: the sensible individuals, the sad or rather dull ones, who take things in stride;

Nature No. 3: The nervous ones push limits and test the cutoff points continuously.

And all the attributes in the middle! Use his parents as a rule because you have probably already made the wise assumption that he is now more like Mom or Dad.

Before you begin, remember that certainty gives your foal faith in you, whereas confusion makes your foal fight or dread. Therefore, make sure you are confident in yourself and what you are doing at each stage of

the way.

This is important; if you are even a little frightened, it will spread to your foal, and you will become a nervous wreck.

Ensure you have a plan for every action or reaction from your foal. Even worse than starting nervously is realizing halfway through and unhinging, creating a problem where none should exist due to novelty.

The Filly

According to the clock, it was two o'clock in the afternoon when Josie woke up. She had taken a four-hour nap. Josie saw as she looked around that this bedroom had an adjoining bathroom.

Josie sprayed water on her face and looked around. She had full use of the spacious bathroom! There was a big bathtub, a separate shower, and a marble basin. Josie would love living in such luxury, even though she knew she would always mourn her mother.

Josie glanced inside Aunt Sue's room as she strolled down the hallway. Josie chose to look around the yard as she was sound asleep.

Perched on the edge of a profound basalt canyon stood the residence. Far down, a brook meandered among towering pines and willows.

Josie believed she recalled where the trail was. It meandered down to the creek, hugging the canyon's edge.

She eventually located the trail's entrance after a few false starts. It was rugged and steep. It appeared that there was a two-hundred-foot drop to the canyon floor. Josie saw numerous broken branches and loose rocks. It appeared as though the trail was hardly utilized.

A few big boulders that had tumbled down the cliff forced Josie to scale them to continue on the trail. She managed to reach the creek without tripping over the sheer cliff face.

She turned around and glanced back up the rugged wall of the canyon. She was only able to glimpse a tiny portion of the house. After she crossed the brook, no one would know she was down there.

How would she cross it, though? The brook resembled a tiny river full of recently melted snow.

Josie went downstream to investigate whether large rocks or fallen logs would allow her to traverse the rapids without wading through.

Eventually, she reached a location where the creek broadened. The modest flow of the brook revealed sand and pebbles as the willows that had been embracing its far bank parted. She could wade to the opposite side without worrying about getting swept downstream if she removed her shoes.

The water in the creek was nearly as chilly as the snow from whence it originated. The water level even reached her ankles at this location as the stream's flow expanded dramatically. When she got to the far side, her feet were a brilliant pink, and she was shaking from the cold.

Josie crossed the area, warmed her feet, and put on her shoes while perched on a big rock.

It was a beautiful, warm day. Josie caught the scent of the aspen trees—sweet and spicy. The roots of the high country, water-loving tree spread out across the mud shoals formed as the creek wound its way from one side of the canyon to the other like spider webs.

Josie felt a profound calmness descend upon her. She had a feeling that things would improve eventually. Subsequently, she perceived the sound of leaves rustling as if being tread upon. It was not the birdsong or the sound of the breeze. It originated in the bushes right behind her. She sat quite quietly, listening once more.

What might that be? She was certain, for whatever reason, that no one was creating the sounds. It has to be an animal, she reasoned. Is that a mountain lion? Was she secure? Was that feeling of calm and well-being a lie?

No, Josie thought to herself. I've gone through enough; God wouldn't do that to me today. She decided to look into the sound's origin as a result. She gently climbed down from the boulder and went through the dense willows to investigate the commotion.

She was shocked by what she saw as she carefully brushed aside the final willow branches. Twenty feet away, a young horse was staring directly at her.

Josie estimated the foal to be four or five months old. It was already around the size of an adult horse, although its tail and mane were still small.

Laying on the ground next to the foal was its mother, or at least what was left of its mother. Josie could see the mare was dead, even at a distance. Josie was relieved to recall that a four or five-month-old foal would have been weaned off of its mother's milk.

Josie muttered, "Oh, you poor thing." "You, too, are an orphan!"

Two big crows landed on the mare's body. The brown and white colt quickly swung around with a low sigh to face the birds. With its forelegs, it lashed out in a charge.

A few yards away, on a large ponderosa pine, the ravens descended and made their landing. "Caw, caw! They taunted the foal, saying Josie took a close look at the baby pinto and saw that it was a filly.

She called him "you sweet thing." "You're attempting to keep your mother safe. You are unaware of her passing.

Nothing is more stunning to witness as a competitor or trainer than a horse and rider collaborating to finish the barrel pattern with complete trust and impeccable accuracy. In hindsight, there's nothing more difficult to witness than a horse and rider having difficulty understanding one another and turning away in frustration, confusion, and rage.

I'm frequently asked how I prepare my barrel horses to compete at the highest levels so quickly and what kind of curriculum I employ. Getting to where I am now as a barrel horse trainer has taken me over thirty years, two hundred horses, and a great deal of trial and error with various training techniques. My training regimen has been honed down to a certain combination of drills and methods that I have found to be effective with barrel horses every time.

Being a visual learner, I discovered that when I was attempting to learn a new training approach, I wanted to see every little detail of how it was done to fully comprehend why it was done. I also learned as a trainer that I could considerably improve the horses' learning process by providing visual aids for myself. I could give the horses more precise and consistent signals—that is, signals that always came simultaneously—when I incorporated visual aids into my workouts. I reduced the amount of time I spent teaching my horses and improved their accuracy and consistency by implementing visual aids into my program.

Thus, when I set out to write this book, I aimed to include as many clear illustrations and training exercises as possible, along with a wealth of written content that explains every step in detail so the reader can grasp it all. I wanted to thoroughly explain the exercises—the why and what for—to help the reader better comprehend how the exercises function since knowing why you are doing something also helps you understand how to do it right.

Visual aids are very beneficial not just to the rider but also to the horse. Since horses are visual learners, you will get better results if you can include visual aids in their training. I discovered that if the horse had some sort of visual aid to help him grasp what I was asking of him, it improved his comprehension of my instructions.

My ability to teach my horses to be more exact and consistent increased when I incorporated visual aids into my training routines and activities. I cut down on training time so much that over the years, I have created a special set of drills and methods that use visual aids for both the rider and the horse. I have produced consistent and successful barrel horses in half the time it used to take me by focusing my training on these special workouts and tactics.

I have dissected the exercises in this book to provide thorough how-to instructions that even a beginner rider can understand. From the beginner to the established professional and the barrel prospect to the finished barrel horse, these training strategies and exercises will assist both horse and rider in developing their communication and riding skills to consistently perform those faultless barrel runs.

Not everyone has the funds or desire to purchase a barrel horse that is already well-tuned. They would like to know how to get the most out of their current horse. This book serves as a how-to guide for all of these competitors in barrel racing. Providing them with the training resources to adjust and maximize the performance of their horses enables them to enhance the horses they now own.

Even though there are a lot of barrel racing books available now, I notice that most of them are about the author and their achievements. There is also very little technical information on how to train and fine-tune a barrel horse because they cover a wide range of barrel racing-related topics, such as breeding, conformation, basic horsemanship, and equipment for barrel horses. These books include almost little about barrel racing concepts or the actual barrel pattern. These books are between 150 and 200 pages long, but only 20 to 40 of those pages provide instructions on how to train your horse or run the barrels properly. As a result, the information is ambiguous and incomplete.

All of these books emphasize the value of consistency, but they don't go into great length about the methods that educate the rider on how to be consistent in training; instead, they advise using repetition to instill consistency in the horse. Even though repetition is an excellent teaching tool, inconsistent repetition simply confuses the horse. Knowing the real barrel pattern is one of the most crucial aspects of barrel racing. None of these publications teaches you how to measure the barrel pockets or provides precise measurements so you can know exactly where to run your horse on the pattern to guarantee the fastest run possible.

While I acknowledge that a barrel horse's genes contribute significantly to its ideal conformation and athletic ability, proper training is necessary for even the best-bred barrel horse to reach its peak performance.

My book breaks down the barrel pattern using mathematics, geometry, physics, and science so that you may work on and fully grasp each element of the barrel pattern, one portion at a time. This sets it apart from other barrel racing books that are currently available. It then walks you through how to utilize that information to decide what and where you and your horse need to work on, with clear, easy-to-follow step-by-step instructions. It also demonstrates how to use that knowledge to address the issues you've found. Lastly, it improves the learning process by providing you and your horse with visual cues to help you run more consistently and accurately while giving orders.

Thirty years of trial and error have taught me what makes a training technique superior to another, which is the basis for the training approaches in this book. The ones that work the best have been maintained, while those that take too long or don't work have been discarded. With these special training methods, I have been able to elicit the best performance possible from my horses and have produced champion after champion in the barrel racing world in a comparatively short time. These workouts and training methods have enabled me to succeed greatly.

Please feel free to share your thoughts about this book with me if you encounter me out on the path. I'm always up for new concepts and resources to add to my knowledge base. There's always something new to learn about training techniques; therefore, you can never know it all. With any luck, this book will help you fill it.

Chapter 2: How Arabian Horses Should Be Maintained

Arabian horses have an edge over other horse breeds since they are native to the Arabian deserts. Their hardy desert habitats have equipped them for almost any kind of weather. Furthermore, their association with people and selective breeding have made them ideal household animals. They are quick learners and very attentive to relationships with humans. When dealing with Arabian horses and developing a partnership, there are still many things to consider, even with their readiness.

The following are some of the key characteristics that set Arabian horses apart from other horse breeds:

Their skeletal structure is delicate. To put it another way, they look stunning.

Their neck has a lovely arch to it.

Their profile is concave.

Their tail is carried high.

These lovely horses are great companions for racing, endurance riding, and other horse sports. They used to only be found in Arabian countries, but these days, they can be found worldwide, including in the US, UK, Australia, Canada, and other places.

There are things you need to do to properly care for your horse if you want them to be healthy. To ensure their wellness, you should provide them plenty of space to live and a place to call home, like a pasture, barn, or run. You have to be adamant about feeding them and giving them access to water regularly, making sure their food gives them the right amount of nutrition for healthy growth and survival. Arabian horses also require appropriate hoof and veterinarian care in addition to this. Grooming and regular exercise are also essential.

There's a misperception regarding tack. Although horses are robust creatures who can care for themselves, proper care requires a lot of work because they are not kept in their natural habitat. All domestic horses, of course, need to be given the right care.

Some of the greatest methods for caring for an Arabian horse will be covered in this chapter. An Arabian horse will treat you with love and affection if you give them the tools they need to succeed. Having a positive relationship with your horse is crucial. You may build this bond by taking good care of him, spending time with him, and showing him love and respect.

Required Basics for Arabian Horses

Arabian horses have certain basic needs that you should always be aware of. Understanding these fundamental requirements will enable you to care for your equine in a way that will guarantee their happiness and, consequently, the mutual benefit of your partnership.

Maintain Your Equine on a Pasture

Your horse's first demand is for comfortable living quarters. Your horse must have access to a pasture of his own. Keeping your horse on a pasture is not hard because it requires little upkeep and money. On the other hand, you shouldn't leave your horse unattended in the pasture for an extended period.

A horse typically needs at least one acre of pasture to graze on. Ensure the pasture has adequate grass in it at all times so the horse can graze easily. In addition, since toxic weeds can pose a major risk to your Arabian horse's health, you should ensure that the pasture is free of them. Some toxic plants are oak leaves, sorghum, ragwort, yew, privet, sycamore, and bracken. To prevent future issues, make an effort to become knowledgeable about the toxic plants in your area.

Here are a few methods you may use to manage the pasture and ensure your horse's safety. These are a few of those methods:

There are numerous places in the nation where horses cannot graze throughout the winter. If you live in a place like this, ensure your horse has access to enough food in the pasture so the winter months won't be a hardship for you. Their health is at stake, even though this may result in greater expenses.

Maintain the pasture's level terrain. Your horse may become uncomfortable standing on uneven terrain for extended periods due to uneven ground. Unusual breathing patterns, rigid neck muscles, pinched ears, tail swishing, grinding teeth, spooking, fidgeting, and foot elevating indicate your horse's discomfort.

Farm equipment shouldn't be kept in the pasture since your horse could easily get injured by something buried in the tall grass.

Avoid keeping any rubbish or unwanted objects in the pasture. Once more, your horse may be at risk if something is concealed by tall grass.

To ensure the horse's safety, a fence should encircle the pasture. There ought to be gates as well. This ensures that the horses don't wander onto other people's land. The fence should stand five to six feet tall, in my opinion.

It is also crucial that the pasture has an appropriate drainage system. The pasture shouldn't have any standing water.

For the horses, always leave mineral or salt blocks in the pasture.

Everywhere, there should be equal grass.

The road ought to be simple to get to.

Behavioral Issues and Training

What precisely are behavioral and training issues?

There has long been a mislabeling of horses. A pony that is in pain, won't comply with our requests, or

acts badly when outfitted has been classified as someone who "needs really preparing or has a conduct issue that necessities revising." Additionally, pony owners have been paying $500 to $1,000 a month to have their ponies "be prepared to act," when it would have been much better for both the pony and your pocketbook to identify and address the physical problems causing the social problems.

Unfortunately, when the pony returns, it usually acts worse than when it went or comes back very sore or weak. I'll explain why in a moment or two.

The story goes that you should run the pony around the field or round pen until they are willing to listen to you and behave the way you need them to, regardless of whether it is torturing them. This is seen in many outbuilding preparations and standard equestrian methods.

But if you pay close attention, you can notice that when a pony is handled free, without a harness or ropes, it will stick its ears or wash its tail in response to being asked to follow a particular developmental path or change directions.

Sadly, the ordinary horsemanship people I have visited are not taking this as seriously as I feel they should. At this point, they are telling us that it is agonizing to move in that way.

It used to happen to me that after only thirty days of retraining, the owners of ponies labeled as risky or difficult would say, "That's not my pony." This pony is calm, well-mannered, and quiet. How did you handle the fabled fire-breathing beast that I left here?

"I simply focused on the pony," I uttered.

"You're one of those "horse whisperers," gracious?"

And I would respond, "No, I paid attention to what the pony needed, fixed the body problems that were making the discomfort worse, brought in an equine dentist to adjust their teeth, and adjusted the hooves to allow for easy and accurate movement of their joints." The horse is glad to comply with my requests when it feels joy, ease, and comfort in its body again.

A pony will misbehave if unhappy and in agony, just as you would if you had real work that upset you and needed to be completed. They are letting you know that they are somewhere in agony. My website offers videos that walk you through finding and fixing the problems on your own. They are not experts! Believe it or not!

Before getting too worked up about your pony's bad behavior under the saddle, I advise having your pony examined by a professional in equine bodywork or pony alignment if you are not ready to dive right in.

You're looking for more than just a horse massage therapist. One problem is that many modalities only address the symptoms; they don't look for or address the underlying cause of the exacerbation. What is meant by that?

Your calves would be sore before the day was done and tight and painful the next day if you had shoes with a worn-out outside edge and went climbing and your foot couldn't land as predicted. However, that's how the pony's legs feel after adjusting to unbalanced hooves.

Imagine that your right shoulder is stiff and not working as it should. Then, you are expected to spend the entire day painting the ceiling or weeding the lawn. Before the day is out, your soreness, exhaustion, and irritability will increase. Imagine having to return for five days in a row and perform the same task repeatedly. This is what happens five days a week while a pony is being lunged and getting ready. If someone asked you to do something repeatedly, five days a week, you would not be polite and probably become agitated. Most likely, you would have to give up! These are our ponies when the side shoulder on that side cannot move precisely due to a twisted first rib. In this sense, they would prefer not to follow that lead around. They won't want to trot to one side in the round pen if the main rib on the right side isn't where it should be, which leads to problems with the right shoulder.

Unfortunately, we have been led astray into believing that this is a deficiency or a readiness problem, and the pony is encouraged to complete more of it until they exhibit the appropriate attitude toward it.

Every time I see that, I grimace. I assume I assume that people will get more educated and discover the cause of the "strange lameness" and the "preparation and conduct issues."

The pelvis, midribs, and shrivels are all pulled out of position by this imbalance, resulting in an irregular horse.

Your pony might provide you with a few enjoyable rides. When you tighten the girth, it will appear angrier, pinning its ears back or swishing its tail. When the circle of a hard, even-molded seat is fixed on a pony's body that is not even-formed, the pony experiences agony and is rendered incapable of moving.

Examine your horse's back form while standing 10 feet behind it on a bucket. You will notice that one side of the rump is higher or more muscular. One shoulder will typically be larger, one side rib will typically be lower, and the withers—where the mane finishes close to the back—will not be straight. However, this horse will pass an equestrian professional's pre-purchase examination.

Now, presuming that the pony is safe to do so, bend down ten feet behind it and look at the back of its hooves. A variety of shapes will be visible, and some areas of the foot will not be rounded as they should be but rather sequential.

You can now see that neither your horse nor the hooves it stands on are symmetrical. This leads to early arthritic diseases and improper joint loading in the body. Usually, before they turn ten years old, unexplained lameness begins to manifest, although, in reality, it's not mysterious lameness.

You can learn the cause of your pony's suffering and how to address these numerous problems at home. If you ever need assistance, don't hesitate to email, skype, or call me or my verified teachers.

The big problem is that the hurting spot isn't where the stuttering started.

The sore spot on the body results from overworking it to make up for a part or area that wasn't initially able to function as intended.

Pay attention to their body, tail, and ears when you get anything done with them. They are going to tell you a story. When someone is riding in a field, observe them asking their pony to do anything that isn't expected of it. Take note if the tail wails in agitation and the ears shift back or stay level.

Do any of these symptoms occur when you place a seat cushion and seat on your pony?

Is your pony happily sleeping while you start to remedy the bigness? Or does it sustain itself, shake its wilts or skin to eliminate bothersome flies, bite, clutch, or wash its tail?

All symptoms indicate excessive disturbing and discomfort.

Adding our weight to the seat on top of it generates more unease, which can cause issues like kicking, walking off while attempting to mount, gnawing at stirrups, not having any desire to trot, or changing leads or diagonal. These are not matters of preparation. These physical issues need to be resolved for the pony and rider to enjoy time spent riding together and for the pony to continue being rideable well into their 30s.

Ponies start to drift apart when they have a calm enough personality and attitude to be okay for your family. What action could you take in this regard?

You can learn a few easy lessons from trained teachers, and I teach you to make your horse happy, obedient, and accident-free.

You may also ensure that your pony lives happily into its 30s by having an equine dentistry specialist with many years of experience—not usually your local veterinarian—check its mouth and teeth for sharp edges and dental problems.

My website, www.holistichorseworks.com, features a ton of recordings that I've made for personal growth. I also provide important distance readings to further diagnose your pony's problems. A six-page PDF report detailing your pony's medical condition is sent to you; it covers solid, skeletal, viral, bacterial, and cerebral problems. Where your pony has been tormented and how to support your horse.

Section 1: Disciplines in English

In horseback riding, there are two primary varieties of saddles: English, or hunt seat, and Western. "English" got its name because it is directly derived from the riding style that was created and made popular in England. When riding over fences and traversing terrain that included hills, valleys, and streams, mounted hunters and cavalry would have an open seat thanks to the design of the saddles.

English riding strongly focuses on the rider's position and efficiency—a concept known as "equitation." Their spine is straight, their chest is open, and their heels are down. However, looks aren't everything. A subtle center of balance, a soft, following arm that makes direct contact with the horse's mouth through the bit, and an almost super-straight, tall spine are all necessary for the very specialized and direct kind of contact that these disciplines entail between the rider and the horse. In actuality, it is the outcome of completely contracted abdominal muscles.

Jumping saddles, in particular, are frequently quite simple hunt seat saddles. The seats are flat, the panels are thin, and the "rolls"—padding at the knees and thighs—serve as a bridge rather than as comfort for the rider and horse's anatomy. The thin stirrup leathers, which appear incredibly delicate and slender, attach the stirrups, often called irons, to the saddle. There isn't a lot of gear between the rider and the horse most of the time.

As a result, novice riders in the English disciplines frequently experience extreme saddle looseness and instability. The secret to making you feel safe and assisting you in staying out of the way of the horse as he moves is to develop a secure seat.

To feel confident, though, requires much confidence and practice. After riding a different discipline for some time, many riders who move to English disciplines say they feel like their legs are swinging erratically. When you sit in an English saddle for the first time, you may feel your spine try to curve into a cozyfetal posture. Your arms and shoulders might clench as you grasp the reins with two white-knuckled hands, and your legs might cling to the horse in fear.

You can feel so exposed and threatened that you give up at that very moment. Permit me to reassure you that every single rider on an English saddle has experienced utter insecurity at some point.

I remember my very first English class. After a year of Western pleasure riding, I realized it wasn't my thing. It wasn't bad, but I wanted to jump, so I had to switch saddles. The horse I rode for my first lesson years prior was the one I rode in an English saddle for the first time. I wanted to ride the easiest horse possible, but my instructor told me I had long since mastered the necessary skills to ride other horses.

We never managed to finish our stroll. My legs lost their intended position when my seat met the strange saddle. My heels gave me a quick lift. My neck instantly froze in terror, taking the rest of my body with it as my hands failed to grasp the short reins. I remained in terror until my teacher requested that we finish the class early or transition to a Western saddle.

I didn't do either. I gradually regained my balance, but my father complained that I walked in circles for an hour, which was expensive. Instead of fighting how my hips moved naturally with the movement of my horse's back, I was learning how to find my place in the saddle. Before long, I was trotting, then cantering, and lastly, I was performing the leaping motion that had initially captivated my attention.

I like to tell my pupils this tale now because I think it's vital to recognize that everyone learns differently. Some people find riding on an English saddle feels very natural, particularly if their horse is stocky and fits them well. However, you could feel quite insecure if you're a petite person riding a narrow horse or the saddle doesn't suit you well.

Remember that there are various levels in each of these sports when you read the descriptions of some common hunt seat disciplines that follow. Before they cross fences, everyone starts over ground poles. Before performing canter pirouettes, all students learn how to stop and salute at X. It's not a reason for shame to be a novice rider; rather, it's reason for great pride that you dared to mount a 1,000-pound quarry in the first place.

Explore the various applications of an English saddle and get some experience!

www.ingramcontent.com/pod-product-compliance
Lightning Source LLC
Chambersburg PA
CBHW052143110526
44591CB00012B/1832